a little book of

hugs™

to
encourage
and inspire

Inspira

Andrews
Publishing

Kansas Cit

ISBN: 0-7407-1187-3

Library of Congress Catalog Card Number: 00-102163

Messages by G.A. Myers
Personalized Scriptures by LeAnn Weiss
Interior design by Vanessa Bearden
Project Editor: Philis Boultinghouse

A Special Gift

presented to:

_____

from:

_____

date:

_____

contents

The spirit, the will to win, and the will to excel are the things that endure. These qualities are so much more important than the events that occur.

—*Vince Lombardi*

chapter one

the
POWER
of
Giving

Don't be selfish
or self-seeking in
anything that you do.

Instead of being self-promoting,
be *humble*
and *consider others*
MORE *important*
than yourself in
all you do and *say*.

Encourage
one another,
and *build*
each other up.

Love,
Jesus

Philippians 2:3; 1 Thessalonians 5:11

When was the last time you felt really warm and loved?

Think about it.

It was probably the last time someone went out of his or her way to do or say something nice to you—something unrequested, out of the blue, just because—something that made you feel valued and appreciated.

And that's how you can make others feel loved—by doing or saying something nice...just because.

So give of yourself
and of your time; give
surprise gifts and
encouraging words.

Take your spouse on a
date and focus all your
attention on your chosen
one. Gather your family
around the kitchen table
and initiate an appreciation
session. Take a friend to
lunch just to remind him
or her that you cherish
that relationship.

Giving is the spark that
ignites the fires of love.
You have the power to
start a blazing fury of
selfless love.

Maturity begins to grow when you can sense your concern for others outweighing your concern for yourself.

—*John McNaughton*

chapter two

2

the
FREEDOM
of
Forgiveness

*G*ood News!
Everyone who *believes*
in **Me** receives
TOTAL *forgiveness*
of sin
through My name.

There isn't
any CONDEMNATION.
Because of what I did at
Calvary, you've been
set *free*
from the law of **SIN**
and **DEATH**.

Your record
has been *wiped* C L E A N.
I *forgive*
and *forget!*

Love,

Your Forgiving
and Forgetting Savior

Acts 10:43;
Romans 8:1–2; Hebrews 10:17

"*You* are forgiven."

Just words? No—much more. The mere utterance of these three little words can free prisoners from guilt in an instant.

$\mathscr{S}$ay the words quietly
to yourself, then speak
them boldly to needy
souls around you.

Graciously accepting
the forgiveness freely
given to us by God, we
are compelled to become
conduits of forgiveness
for others.

Someone near you
needs forgiveness today.
You hold the power to
free that person.

If the offense was committed against you, remember your own undeserved forgiveness; draw from that abundant supply and share what has been given to you— it is not yours to hoard.

If the offense is against someone else, speak a word of testimony about God's loving forgiveness and encourage actions that lead to healing.

Forgiveness releases others from their indebtedness to us and releases us from our indebtedness to them— both freed to love.

You have been given a
precious power. Receive
and give it generously and
often.

&

Our God has
a big eraser.

—*Billy Zeoli*

Ho**w** magnificent is grace! How sweet are the promises! How sour is the past! How precious and broad is God's love! How petty and narrow are man's limitations! How refreshing is the Lord!

—*Charles Swindoll*

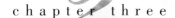

chapter three

3

the
SECRET
of
Acceptance

Practice humility
toward one another.

I *oppose* the **PROUD**.

But I give My
A M A Z I N G
grace
to those
who are HUMBLE.

Love,
Your God Who Is Gentle
and Humble in Heart

1 Peter 5:5

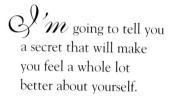

I'm going to tell you
a secret that will make
you feel a whole lot
better about yourself.

It's something you've allowed yourself to consider before...but not for very long.

The very essence of this secret will make you bristle, even though you know that accepting it will ease your mind, calm your spirit, and even whet your appetite for growth.

*A*re you ready? I know you can handle it, though not everyone can. Here goes:

You are not always right.

I saw you smile,
because you know I'm
right—well, about this,
anyway.

Trying to be right about everything is a load you cannot carry, and the cost is far more than you can afford.

The next time you look in the mirror, you may want to remind yourself of this secret.

And I'll tell you another secret: Admitting that you're not always right makes you even more lovable than you already are—if that's possible.

God created the world out of nothing, and so long as we are nothing, he can make something out of us.

—*Martin Luther*

chapter four

the
ESSENCE
of
Courage

Be full of STRENGTH
and *courage*.

Do not be *terrified;*

do not be discouraged.

I will be *with you*

wherever

you go.

Love,
Your God of
Strength and Courage

Joshua 1:9

Would you
describe yourself as a
person of courage?
Probably not.

Your image of courage may have been shaped by television and movies: Courage is Superwoman flying to rescue a helpless child from a burning building.

Or perhaps it's Will Smith saving the world from aliens who plan to destroy us and confiscate our natural resources.

Make-believe courage
is hard to live up to. But
real courage, in real life,
may describe you to a tee.

It takes courage to care about family and friends enough to get involved with their struggles. It takes courage to complete what you start. It takes courage to confront weakness in your own life and in the lives of those you love.

It takes courage to confess that your thoughtless words or negligent actions have hurt someone you love. Quite simply, it takes courage to live each day with integrity.

You may not describe yourself as a person of courage, but look again— you may discover courageous feats of kindness or heroic manifestations of unconditional love.

*S*ay, would you like
to be in a movie?

Courage is
fear that has said
its prayers.

—from
One Day at a Time,
Al-Anon

chapter five

the RICHES
of *Memories*

I want you to think about
whatever is **true**.

Think about things that are
NOBLE or *RIGHT*...
things that are
pure *and lovely*.

Reflect upon
ADMIRABLE qualities and
memories.

Remember

whatever is
EXCELLENT or
praiseworthy.

Love,
Your God of Every
Good and Perfect Gift

Philippians 4:8

You may not
realize it, but you are
a rich person. Yes, you!
You possess a huge vault
brimming with treasure,
and you can withdraw
assets from this vault
whenever you want—at
absolutely no cost.

Where is this vault?
It is inside the caverns
of your heart and mind.
And what treasure
resides there?
 Memories.

$\mathscr{M}$emories are pictures of past events and people that powerfully affect your present and future. There are those funny memories from long ago that make you laugh, even now.

Then there are those
embarrassing memories
that flash through your
mind at the oddest times,
even causing you to blush.

But there are certain kinds of memories that glisten like diamonds. They remind you that your life is rich with meaning and purpose— that you matter to other people and that other people matter to you.

Memories of special moments when love was exchanged and cherished, when a significant relationship took a big step forward, when delicious laughter cheered your soul—these precious memories are all waiting for you to pick them up, dust them off, and bring them to life once again.

So when your heart is
heavy or you're feeling
all alone, open the
door…go ahead. Dig in.
Make all the with-
drawals you want.

You can't deplete the supply. In fact, you may find that you are so rich you can loan some of your wealth to others.

Enjoy yourself.
These are the good
old days you are going
to miss in ten years.

—*Unknown*